SCRIMSHAW

SCRIMSHAW

"The term scrimshaw comes from an old word, 'scrimshander' or 'scrimshanker,' meaning an idle, worthless fellow. The term gradually came to mean the objects made by a sailor during his idle time at sea. Scrimshaw is the only indigenous American folk art, aside from that of the Indians."—*Bulletin No. 43, Marine Historical Association, Inc., Mystic, Connecticut, 1949–1950.*

"Scrimshaw is folk art devised by whalemen. . . . It represented the striving of men, exiled on long whaling voyages, to attain something beautiful with the crude implements and materials at hand."—*Z. W. Pease, in* The New Bedford Mercury, *2 December, 1920.*

"Throughout the Pacific, and also in Nantucket, and New Bedford, and Sag Harbor, you will come across lively sketches of whales and whaling scenes, graven by the fishermen themselves on Sperm Whale-teeth, or ladies' busks wrought out of the Right Whale-bone, and other like skrimshander articles, as the whalemen call the numerous little ingenious contrivances they elaborately carve out of the rough material, in their hours of ocean leisure. . . . Long exile from Christendom and civilization inevitably restores a man to that condition in which God placed him, *i.e.,* what is called savagery. . . . As with the Hawaiian savage, so with the white sailor-savage. With . . . his one poor jack-knife, he will carve you a bit of bone sculpture, not quite as workmanlike, but as close packed in its maziness of design, as the Greek savage, Achilles's shield. . . ."—*Herman Melville, in* Moby-Dick, *1851.*

SCRIMSHAW

BY

Winfield Townley Scott

PS
3537
C943S3

C 1463

THE MACMILLAN COMPANY
NEW YORK 1959

Copyright © Winfield Townley Scott 1949, 1950, 1951, 1952, 1953, 1954, 1955, 1956, 1957, 1959

"Watch Hill," previously published in *discovery no. 5* under the title "unsexed by the cold sea," Copyright © 1955 by Pocket Books, Inc.

"Two" (page 47), Copyright © 1957 The New Yorker Magazine, Inc.

All rights reserved—no part of this book may be reproduced in any form without permission in writing from the publisher, except by a reviewer who wishes to quote brief passages in connection with a review written for inclusion in magazine or newspaper.

The author thanks the editors of the following publications for permission to reprint most of the poems in this book: *The Atlantic, The Beloit Poetry Journal, California Quarterly, Coastlines, Contemporary Poetry, Dilliman Review, discovery no. 5, Epoch, The Hopkins Review, Inscape, The Nation, The New Orleans Poetry Journal, The New Mexican, The New Mexico Quarterly, The New Republic, New World Writing, The New Yorker, Nucleus, Partisan Review, Poetry* (Chicago), *Saturday Review, The Virginia Quarterly,* and *The Western Review;* and the editors of several anthologies that collected some of these poems before the author could: *Fifteen Modern American Poets* (Rinehart), *Mid-Century American Poets* (Twayne), *New Poems by American Poets* (Ballantine Books), *Poet's Gold* (Devin-Adair), and *Three Self-Examinations* (Beloit Chapbook). The poem "Memento" was read before the Alpha Chapter, Phi Beta Kappa, Brown University, March, 1954.

First Printing

Printed in the United States of America

The Macmillan Company, New York
Brett-Macmillan Ltd., Galt, Ontario

Library of Congress catalog card number: 59-13508

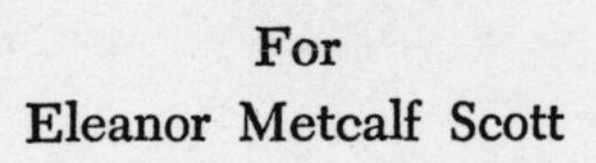

For
Eleanor Metcalf Scott

Contents

1: Come Green Again

All Memory

The trees smoke with fog.
Old ghosts around me.
After the rain spoke warm air, cold ground,
Slow, coastal wind,
Woke these, but not to walk;
To talk what I recall.

Stand stiff in their stirring robes
Like that host of men in my dream
Who stared blind and silent
Toward the shuttered sea;
And now surround me.
Hooded, faceless, listening.

O ghosts, stay round me!
Soft is this guttural utterance
Of spring. And the mutter
Of the rain renewed in fog
Darkens. Unlost, all memory
Subsides to this stillness.

Come Green Again

If what heals can bless
Can what blesses heal?
And all come green again
That was bodied forth
Years and years ago?
Years before my time.

Yet things I deepest learned
Turn into memory
As though no man's creation
But enlarges mine;
As though no man's existence
But was also mine
In its lonesomeness.

Henry Thoreau bent
In his boat on Walden Pond
Whistling his wooden flute
Under midnight stars
Across the stars in the water.

Hawthorne and Melville parting
At night in Liverpool,
Parting on a rainy corner
For the final time,
Something unsaid between them.

Mark Twain in moonlight
Standing in his Hartford house,
That wounded, beautiful man,
His hands at his white hair
While he sang "Nobody knows
The troubles I see but Jesus."

Then in broad daylight
The ladies of Camden drawing
Their skirts and kids aside
To avoid the dirty man
As Whitman hobbled past,
His basket on his arm
Filled with his book for sale.

Can such existences
Help but heal our hearts
Or such lonesomeness
Help but bless in us
That everlasting change
Which is our changelessness
And our humbleness?
And all come green again.

What I have learned enough
To have as air to breathe
Returns as memory
Of undiminished love:
That no man's creation
But enlarges me.
O all come green again.

The Difference

The buffalo loomed at the far loop of the field:
Though mildly grazing in twilight, a thunderhead tethered.
Spectators—man and two children—some others—
Clutched tickets and kept their distance, regarding the rare beast.

We were—after all—suddenly there—there in the same grass
At the edge of our town: the familiar vacant lot
Usurped by the savage shape which grazed inattentive:
We grew—embarrassed, frightened—into shy invaders.

Staring and silent, we stood back. Though the crickets rang
And the evening star opened low over the western fence
The shadowy field was bisontine; the ground shook—
Once—with the thud of an absent-minded forefoot.

The little girl said to her father "I want to go see him";
But the boy dared not: he watched them hand in hand
Go slowly within the dusk to confront—quite close—
While he stayed alone among strangers—that hunching darkness.

Silhouette now: the buffalo: horned ghost
Of an ancient philosopher, bearded and ominous,
Transmigrated, neither free nor dead. Nothing occurred
To the father and sister. They returned safe. The three went
home.

Wax

A covey of cotton-dressed, apple-breasted girls
Squealed from the hut as the two boys crossed the field
And were gone when the boys reached the hut,
Entered and saw the wax thing on the floor.

Not a candle. By projecting themselves
Immensely (so it seemed to them) older,
The boys knew—there in the damp shadows
Of musty ruins—what the replica was.

Glans end hung broken on the central string.
Half as thick as their wrists the thing made
A frightening excitement when their thin fingers
Explored the hard rod of dirty yellow.

They hid it under a rotted floorboard,
Not knowing why they hid it, any more
Than they imagined why, unlike themselves,
The girls had not merely touched for future luck.

Merrill's Brook

Sun over all and air over all and clover
Ripens with bees the summer afternoon
Where pasture right angles at the slanted oak
And swirls the narrow brook to a round brown pool.

The banks are skin-shiny with twenty boys
That flicker warm light into the shade and out,
Running. They leap to a hang of rope and swing
Above the water, let go with a shouting plunge.

The larger and skillful revolve their bald behinds
On a wheel of headover diving, and here jounce
Beginners flouncing, one foot careful in shallows,
Dog-paddlers, and ankle-deep a little brother

Who stands blondly glistening, unspoken-to.
One anxious mongrel circles among the bathers
Who jump back and forth, amphibious of June:
The air's white-knived with knees and shoulder-blades.

Or loll in grass; and now and then pair off
To hide in alder thickets with hot hands,
Emerging red to dive—the hurried thud
Of racing bare-soled on bluet-bevelled earth.

So on so on a hundred summer days
Till the stranger, the stout and hairy Adam, came
With soap and a pleading smile and called to us
While we scrambled to clothes and ran and ran away.

The Ghost

Beyond grown taller pines there's the same house.
Below the house the pond, shrunken by drought,
Is pocked with red and yellow leaves. The silence
Webs from the locked doors and curtained windows,
The stilled pond, the weeds where gardens were,
My hesitance to speak what I do not know,
And failure of anticipated ghosts.
The absent strangers who possess this house
Are nearer, being unknown, than my lost friends.
Intruder on today, I see no summer
Fleshed with naked bodies at the shore,
Nor hear on the cold terrace liquored laughter.
Under its corner draught a clutch of leaves
Circles like wounded bats scratching the stones.
A disused theater, expectant of others
Who needn't care, for there's no mark of us.
My friend the architect of this house is dead,
Those who loved and built, divorced, dispersed,
The Pan-pipes child changed to a man somewhere.
So, what I came for is not here, and it
Departs with me who hoped one revenant
And fetched the wind spiralling in my ribs
And pallor of clouding sun thin through my hands.

Dead Leaves Out of Place

If I return to walk these woods
It is to walk a memoir of desire
Along the lake shore and the hill of pine,
November noon; waters in a pallid sun,
Hillslope under the pine strewn
With a sift of beech leaves, blown from
Some other hill, here strange and the pine
Made strange; blink of a cold day.

Grayed at the rocky edge the lake's seulette
Lips the wind; it is a thinned way
I return amidst promise of ice and
Some recollection as of an illness
Making the place important:
Adolescent delirium, joy and terror,
Lust's invention and the real fever—
Tremor of sun over these dry-bright leaves.

I remember the girl, as one
Reminded of his forgotten poem
Blushes for fabrication, yet may be
By history touched a little; retrospective love
Fulfills itself with a later stranger—
Requires the stilled woods, the skinned mirror,
Knowledge that wherever they belong
Leaves like these return to live again.

Chapter Two

Listen—I'll say you a
Park in the city, a
Park in the dusk just
As the snow is beginning:
The gray-blue, the sweet-cold, the
Whispering rustling.

And

—Do you remember?—
Floor by floor the lights rising
As darkness filled up
The tall wells of the streets
Gigantically ringing the
Small empty park where
The thin snow slid in
As if it would fall
Through the dusk there forever,
Amidst gears', horns' wrangles
Hushing a circle;
The gray-white, the sweet cold.

Oh

—Now you remember—
How young and unhappy and
Lovely you were
How uselessly in
Love we were; and there
Walking alone in New York in the snow
You had nobody anywhere to see to
Talk to nowhere to go.

Summer Place

I think of that summer place where the catalpa flowers
 were chock with sun,
Tree-full, leaf-lifted over the low roof until they were
 stormed to the grass;
They lay like a spendthrift of gnomish orchids surfed from
 a world too small for us to see.

We walked on them. We observed in a day their brown-vein
 stain. Shriveled, they were gone soon
With all such flakes of light that make May and June so far
 from bean-stretching August
Wherein we can better remember—do begin to remember—
 October, December, can never June or May.

We were young then. Summer did not go by—it stood huge
 on the house and in the fields
As if, despite our remembrance, an unbudgeable heat held us;
 and in water-scented nights
For its brief relenting we danced our stripped-down dances
 beneath the black plaques of the tree.

But it did go. Fall flew us away. We were confused with
 seasons, are chilled by so many years.
I imagine the house now as I never saw it at all: stark in
 leafless light and weathered shutters locked,
The crackling sound of someone walking across the crinkled
 pods strewn on the ground.

In That House Where Day Was Night

for W. H. Gerry

Now the old dream comes again.
The stone house in streaming rain
Beyond rain-thickened trees, beyond
Wet-dark wall and the blinded pond;
And I the unseen man shut in.

So my day-dream comes again
And as if time had stopped. No less
That I would not believe or bless
Rained-out sun and the clock locked
In a perpetual usufruct
Which, breathless that I breathed upon,
Left me both living and alone.

Yet the dream grows; the tempest gust
Wild on the roof where I am housed
Safe and sure and safe and sure.
The utmost tree roots can endure
Chaining the wrathful writhe of trees,
Thunder exploding in the chimneys
And the blank endless roar of rain
Upon the cannoned ground—their strain
Proves all my peace and certitude,
Their war my wall.

But for what good
Strides like a stranger in the dream
My friend who died? But now I seem
To remember he believed in rain—
Days of his living communication—
Also that he would break death down
And speak through ashes under stone.
"Cary! Cary!" I call; but pale,

Smiling, cheerfully wistful still,
Across the woods he walks and blurs.
The chilled rain on my face answers.
I close the door for my disbelief
As I had opened it for grief,
And turn away.

The day-dream has
Become a whirl of silences,
Vortex of blacked-out memories.
I cannot say *When was I? Who was*
I? am I? —Where are they gone
Who knew my name? And with a long
Cloud-driven crash the storm attacks
The stone house, and the house cracks
Open to the cracked-open night,
Wind flecking the trees with starlight.

Stars weave among each other over
The windy woods, and I remember
"Nothing that sounded once is lost."
Voices of living man and ghost
Arriving on the withering air
Expand the welkin where they are,
And move and are, and recklessly
Dissolve and die, arise and die,
Re-form in coldest night, rehearse
The unbraiding and braiding universe.

Point of View

for George Loveridge

The man on the roof, his back against the chimney,
Spies as unseen as though he were not there,
Or had been there a quarter-century;
anyway, evening
Starts to come up the street, whispering first
In the bicycle wheels of the boy who lights the lamps
Who whistles from corner to corner, diminuendo—
Gone under the stride of Baby Shea
On whose policing bulk the bluish light
Flat-foots the shadowy concrete. There's a hint of mist.

The sky shifts altogether west now, drops for all
But Mr. Pitman. His incessant cane
Knocks and knocks the pavement and where he climbs
By counted steps safe to his memorized door.
The lamp his little hunch-backed sister lights
Smoulders a medicine that lets him breathe.
The wall closes and evening seems to pause.

Around the corner comes Mr. McGillicuddy,
But blind-drunk only, and down on his knees he flops
Fumbling at the picket gate, calling his daughters.
"Ah," shouts the unseen man against the chimney,
"McGillicuddy, it's always the way this hour:
You think it's the old gate of your childhood home
And misremember the latch. It's the other side."
But nobody hears him, and the favorite daughter
Lugs the old man in.

Sighing the twilight blurs
Arrival of Mr. Barker in the side street,
Hurrying late from the hardware shop to home
Hidden in snowball bushes behind the hedge.

Presently he will stuff the kitchen doors
With all the repetitive read-out newspapers,
Turn on the unilluminating gas
And lie down patiently. But Mrs. Barker
With usual competence will arrive home too early.

In the gray-shingled house to eastward, death
Has just occurred to Toshie Weaver's mother.
Black-gloved, his plump and middle-ageing hands
Project a moment in the helpless dusk
And creak the shutters closed.

Looking up,
Looking like Mark Twain, old Mr. Kaull
Clatters tin watering-can on the slate stoop,
And to the man above him by the chimney
The air around that beautiful white head
Spouts with a magic trick of Audubon cards,
Gifts of his kindness, fixed and singing birds
Which never need perch on Murphy's forbidden trees
High-fenced above Kaull's garden, but will ring
This childish air, bright even in rising fog,
Between the schoolhouse and the harbor horns.

Through the chimney Mrs. Sharwell's voice
Feebling reciting Mary Baker Eddy
Reedily conjures up another room
Into which, it says, she soon will gladly pass.
Clamor of two children resisting bedtime
Sounds from the second floor and then subsides.
And now it is nearly dark.

The corner street-light
Grows taller and keeps humming to itself.
Two backyards to the north the night whirls spiced
With Captain Pearson's peonies; though which
Are pink and which are white—

but now between
This yard and that the foggy scarves float up
Fragrance of the Wilbars' clematis,
A drenching sweetness where a woman walks
Straight-backed the gray-brick path, across the lawn,
And roves from fence to fence, gripping the four,
Confirmed that all are stout as they were made
So long ago. She glances toward the chimney
Of the next roof, and as she turns away
And fades absorbed in darkness, fireflies
Spatter softly before her where she moves
And float a traveling glimmer at her feet
Over the hidden grass.

And now the night
Shuts down with fog, and all the houses drift
As in a tide that sinks them under the sea.

Friday So Soon

There were many people on the island
Though, looking back at it now, it seems we were
Mostly alone together; we were allowed
The customary two weeks; the first
Floated like a slowed dream, like those boats
Windless and weightless and mirrored
Within folded lusters of air. The sea—
It is strange how at once on the island
You forget sea as the way of travel: others'
Continual arrival and disappearance
Enclosed us—safely, we thought, while
The sea-way which bore and must take us
Became God's moat to keep us.
We played in and out of it repeatedly.
Along shore that grass we almost sank in.
Weather spiralled from the full moon: storm
Shot rain and spray in salt horizontals
Three days. There was that too. Yet afterwards
The evening star like a pinwheel nail
Set all the galaxies awhirl until
Our island spun among them—
And then the sun with its wide quietness
Covered the sky and sea. The last days
Grew tense with being last: for instance,
Time and desire for swimming nearly vanished. We
Looked from sea at the grass and trees and flowers.
We were stilled by a recollected plan.
Sometimes I think I must have imagined it all
And yet how real you seemed when we ran with the sea.

Memento

Bessie Townley Scott, 1885–1952

1

This is a rocksaw seacoast.
Puddingstone lugs the thud of glacial death.
Nevertheless the thin earth of the clifftops
Hedges with wild roses the summer sea,
And I say this headland is for us forever
The sheriff of the morning star.

Far down there are cave-cuts where high tide
Jets a commotion of foam.
The sterile wear is slow is
A spoon of pearled emerald from a hundred years.
Yet eastward at evening the ocean
Takes credit for the moon.

Cow-sound foreign there our bell-buoy gonged
Tins and tans; off Brenton Reef
Our lightship makes a medallion.
We have chained these things and now
Would see them only if they disappeared.
We are if we touch the waters a skirl of snow.

Though I have seen navies, vicious though ours,
Soundless past these islands, out of this bay,
Curve toward Gibraltar;
I have imagined dragon-headed ships
Arriving here ten centuries out of port
Loom in marine erasure of history.

Cantilevered into surf this coast
Juts nonhuman; graves of shipwrecked were
Hurricane-gouged; but the swallows
Fly in and out of the earth, fly through

Plunges of gulls that rise
White, shadowed, and white in the dulcet sun.

And I say of these weathers I choose
A seamless afternoon—mansion of glass
As huge as childhood—sea and sky: I say
For an ancient anchor grass-grown
This wreath of roses between stone and salt air
Is breath of the dead whose memories now are mine.

2

Will you hear that I spoke these stones and trees,
These stones under trees, trees over the houses,
These streets and walks, these dooryards hedged and fenced
In the old way, this little town?

I say, without my voice this is all lost, it is nothing.
But I am the passionate marriage of memory and love
And which of you knows even my name or my voice?
How could you know today is today having forgotten
Yesterday and tomorrow.
                                        Yet—whether
You hear or know—I speak; I say that here
Night pours westward off the back of the world
And the sea pours out the sun which rising
Shafts with its tiers of escalators
The moist streets of the morning;
                                                and the streets
Fill with fathers, skip with schoolchildren,
They hush for cool cobbledy sound of horse and wagon
Somewhere around the corner and coming nearer;
They are lanes between lines of washing hung to dance
Over mothers and babies and sandboxes till noon.
Till I say *Sleep*. It is three o'clock. The sun
Inaccessible hovers a while stilled.
No footsteps—no door—no doorbell—all is emptied.
I alone stand, a fixed dream, and watch

That piazza opening through its leafless vines
And the wind in the rockingchair.

3

This lady's memory of these things is gone.
Of us and sixty-seven years her knowledge
Is gone. While you stare down at her long-loved face
The nonexistence which shakes you is your own.

Now you have come to stare at the statue of death
Its terror is in your recognition of it and,
Unlike a real statue, its failure to change,
Its inability to respond. And this conceived you.

From what you know, from what you can bear to see
This must be buried soon. And only for you
Now and always light is everywhere altered,
All the colors of the world are otherwise.

Whom do the mourners see? A girl—a ghost—
A bride—an old and tired lady—a stranger?
They pause and make her momentary replica.
Whom do the mourners see? Themselves. Themselves.

As wave into wave, so memory into memory
Folds, falls forward, follows till some far
And unimaginable coast receives forever
The final landfall of oblivion.

You remember fright and agony were here
But pain cannot be posthumous for her.
The burial signal is thunder and rain. Say *Sleep.*
Sleep, lady: no longer remember even me.

4

Psyche whose threnodic hands
Wash the winter darkness white

Move between the stars and starlight
Where the worlds are whirled to sands
Where all music disappears,
All the answers which we know
Less than shadow less than echo,
The emolument of tears
Turned immaculate fall of snow
Turned anonymous design
Strict as stars that as they fell
Fell unrecognizable,
Now no longer think to tell
Which were hers and which were mine,
Now no further realize–
Psyche whose threnodic hands
Heal the cicatrice of years–
What had soothed her hands and eyes.
Move between the sun and sunrise.

5

Again and yet again midsummer night
Hangs the prismatic curtains of the moon
Draping as with stilled and visible winds
The ocean's quietly dancing arches, leaping
Point Judith to Brenton Reef and to Sakonnet
And sweeping past Aquidneck's phosphorent roofs
Stands in this lifting light on the great bay
And all its shadowy islands: Conanicut,
Gould and Rose and north to Coddington Cove
The twisted whale of Prudence Island–fixed
As in a mindless memory of love.

The moonlight seems to shudder. It is the sea's
Intermittent pausing pulse, its flicker
Of nerves, that shudder. And even these remote
As a sleeping face watched dimly in a mirror;
Watched carefully as though it might awaken
Although I know it will only disappear

And the emptied glass swirl to bluish fog
Quick to be lost in the moon's nameless color.
Although I think that deep within these waters
Stares the figurehead of a nameless lady
Whose long farewells speak from her lidless eyes.

Now this wide glass of sea is voyageless.
The lightship blinks for nothing. The bell-buoy
Bangs for danger of emptiness and home.
At the cliffbase the tide is a caress,
Neither impersonal nor aggressive now
But in an alien armistice feigning peace.
This headland now embodied by the dead
Moves in the kinship of the moon which is
A memory of light and which is love,
And gifted with roses' wild recurrent grace
Sets forth toward day on the rugosa sea.

2: Two Lives and Others

Two Lives and Others

Beyond the field where crows cawed at a hawk
The road bent down between oaks, pines, and maples,
Maples skimming the air with terra cotta.
The oaks spat acorns over scurries of squirrels.
Moss crunched stiff underfoot, and overhead
The sky was freezing gradually, white across blue.
We hurried our walk through shadows, yet it was
A noticeable sort of afternoon:
We honored a faded robin and considered
The importance of the color gray on bluejays.
A woodchuck, all an urgent clumsiness,
Made his tumbling run, then he saw us,
Plunged, hid, and screamed his whistle of fear.
Round the next bend to twilight we went past
A solitary house, one room lamplighted,
An old man at supper alone facing the wall.
If he was aware of us he gave no sign.
We circled home, that last day before snow.

Into the Wind

The child grabbed my hand and made me run with him
Under the slate-dark sky in air chill with grape.

So much November night came rushing toward us
From all four quarters while he danced and sang
As if for a spring morning, and while he ran
A so determined undirected way, I was amazed
To hear him ask where we were going, and could only say
Just before I lost him, "Not all the way together."

I heard his diminishing steps and then the wind.

Then the clouds commenced shifting arrangements of light
Of the cold and mensal, unmentionable moon.

The Last One

Now all that name are gone:
Friends and relatives
Summoned—but left to come
Are nurses, acquaintances.

This neutral ground opened
To be engaged as grave
Arrests the fatiguing air
Which only strangers breathe.

In ninety years she suffered
All other graves nearby:
Now joins them unattended
By lives of memory.

Though undisturbed by her
And the unrequested flowers,
Her long-experienced dead
Reciprocally cease.

The Mother

Bowed down she turned but, halfway up the stairs,
Broke over—fingers, gray head, on the banister.
She cried out: "Everyone I met today
Had someone to take care of them but me.
Everyone wishing me a Merry Christmas,
Then I come home to this dark and empty house.
Aren't you two children grown enough by now
To know what it's been to bring you up alone,
Earn every cent it took? And you don't give
A damn to be with me on Christmas Eve."
And we stood frightened there, seeing her cry
For the first time: deserted, shamed to be
Shamed by having not known what we did,
And seared by shame and pity then we cried
For the first time since we were children, and
She hurried down to us and put her hands
On both our shoulders and said "Oh, my dear boys!
What did I do wrong to hurt you so!"

Mrs. Severin

Mrs. Severin came home from the Methodist Encampment,
Climbed naked to the diningroom table and lay down.
She was alone at the time but naturally told of it afterward.
"Lord! Lord!" she had called out. "Thou seest me. Wherein is
my fault?"

When she heard of it, second-hand, Mrs. Birchfield laughed till
she cried.
"My God!" she said, "I'd like to've seen her getting up there!"
For Mrs. Severin, you see, was a very stout old lady,
A spilling mass by buttons, shawls, pins and ribboned eyeglasses
held together.

The eyeglasses were a shift of drama: hoisted for reading aloud,
lowered for talking;
They were not interruption. Mrs. Severin's soft incessant sibilance
Through all the days she visited and rocked by the window
Braided inextricably Bible and autobiography. Jesus was near.

"The morning Encampment began the Lord suddenly told me to
go.
Ran all the way down-street to the cars for Canobie Lake,
Didn't fasten my dress or tie my shoes. Left the house open.
Young ones at the neighbors.
'Lord,' I said, 'I am thy servant'—and stayed the whole beautiful,
blessed week."

On the listening child her showers of quotation pattered a
drugged dream.
" 'Thought becomes word. Word becomes act. Act becomes char-
acter. Character becomes destiny.'
Remember that. And praise the Lord," she said, giving off also
Odor of camphor, old rose jars and muttonleg sleeves. "Amen!"

The husband long gone who wasted her inheritance; the irritable
children

Who hated to have to have her now; the friends who took her in now and again: gone.
Here in her false hair and handmedowns, patiently talking—talking:
Old Mrs. Severin who once, brave on a diningroom table, naked confronted her unanswering Lord.

Codicil For Pvt. John Hogg's Will

Gray and blue, the boy ghosts with guns are in the spring woods:
Now—a century after—they are here.
West, the Blue Ridge is a line of march along the sky and
into the sky—
A memorial—
And those wide miles of fields roll up to it as though with
love, for the fallacy is always pathetic;
But in these woods, poignant with April, the boys in a mist
that makes the morning old
Rove in a haunt of spring. One can see why.

Sunshine, thin and young, burning like mirrored light, probes
the hepatica-broken leaves
And blankets of violets flung to the gray ground
And windless moss furled on the cedars
And the brook living shyly amidst embracing, stumbling,
fallen trees.
There's bloodwort, brief blossoming.

So youth, one hears, died here long ago.
By the five-toned mourning dove—not only, not alone; no less
Weave of sparrow, waxwing, finch, and cardinal birdsong,
daylong birdsong,
Riddling, caroling chorus through the slowly opening day.

One, a stranger from among the victors if there are victors,
can see why
This could be held dearest of all and to be fought for,
Here in the willow way
Dogwood's ivory stairs to nowhere,
The deep flowering judas.

Phelps Putnam

He twirled his tabled highball. Darkening,
The room minced back and forth in shadows and
His glass I noticed was a child's tumbler
Dappled with a painted pony rockered.

I wondered how it came there. "If my heart
Were strong enough to write again," he said.
"But doctors–." Then he shrugged his old-young face
And poured more whisky in my jelly-glass.

"One can be legendary even at forty,"
He said, "but that is to be alive only
In other people's pasts." He lit the lamp
With careful down-adjustment of the wick.

The tall bookcases righted themselves but all
The uncommunicative countryside
Pressed against the blackened windows closer;
As though a vacuum listened. "If I could

Remember," he remarked. "When I was young
Why, all of us were going to be great men."
He let his drink stand by the lamp and thought.
I looked away. "But to recall one's self,"

I heard him say, "–such ruthless appetite."
Projected from the glass the light had made
The painted toy gigantic–shadow of horse
Massive, silent, living, real, on the wall.

Re-Run

I was that dancer. On the screen
Dances again who once was I
Head Grecian-curled and lean, the lean
Pectoral hardness and his hard thigh

Strident across the film in great
Loves of leaping, in whirls, in slow
Erectile pause of weightless weight
Perfected twenty years ago.

They often re-run. I save to sit
And spy upon the youth who had
Youth without its opposite,
Promise therefore that went bad.

See how he dances ignorance
Of childhood and of you and me;
Half-naked, full magnificence,
He spins before a moonlit sea

Whose tones orchestral and perverse
Whisper, snarl on the sound-track;
But all are caught around those terse
Hips and within that stallion back

To stiff finalities of strength
Feet thundering at the horn's cry,
Until the plot extrudes its length
When in the movie he can die.

Celebrity

Take this jeweled hand but do not hold it:
We bear to be touched momentarily if at all.
This palm has held London and Paris once
And this, New York. You that have never had it
Cannot conceive the weariness of triumph,
The unrelinquishable weariness.
There are in the world similar hands—a few;
We avoid meeting; such weight is unmanageable.
You, we perceive, being jeune and intelligent
May in turn perceive our graciousness bends.
The habits of greatness are so swiftly learned
Yet stay unalterable, my dear young man.
Oh yes, we need you. Let us admit we need you
Everywhere momentarily. Be numerous.
But never allude to others' indiscretions
In all those memoirs which insinuate
The sort of bread these hands once broke upon
And what haired thighs these stiffening fingers stroked.
How much we must forget to smile, to sleep!
The more you think you know the less you know,
And even this we have said you have imagined.
We who were young, poor, arrogant, insurgent,
Are—what else can we say?—are old and famous.

William Primrose Gets His Guarnerius

No fiddle of morning:
All the light in it
Is traveled.

Guarnerius Viola
Shaped of a woman's body,
Three centuries,
Burnished maple;
The night tone shining.

Her silence and sleep so long
Webbed beneath strung starlight.

But William,
Barefooted in kilts to school,
Kind-fathered past jungles of billboards,
Believing in the resurrection,
Traveled humbly toward her,
Grew into the dark forest, the night tone,
Wordless with music.

Now his face bends upon her,
His bow and fingers move:
From interference of learned mortal love
Across far-traveled light
All hymns arise and sing
Human and deathless.

To awaken this
Required
No ordinary prince.

Frieda 75

She opened her eyes, and green
They shone, clear like flowers undone
For the first time, now for the first time seen.
—D. H. Lawrence

Frieda is the old grandma in the fairy tale
In her magic house deep in the German woods.
Why is her house magic? Frieda lives there.
She bends over pots and pans, stirring and tasting
Wonderful broths for all the children who come.

Listen, she laughs like bells all over the room.
That is because there are tears in the broth she stirs.
She traveled a far way to arrive at her house,
Of course leaving much behind her, and learned about tears.
Drink what she has and you'll tell the truth forever.

Like any nice white-haired grandma in the world
She will trot out her jewelbox and show you things:
A necklace and maybe a huge ring from Lorenzo.
What Frieda really wears are a man's words.
That's the magic. She opens her eyes and green they shine.

Just Before the Hurricane

Said the old woman to the young woman, "Darlin
Are ye a whisky drinker? I am myself.
It helps me keep this fist doubled and ready.
Ah, it's pull your punches and no fights for art,"
Said the old woman under her sag of hair.

Said the old woman, "Now it's nobody hurt.
But what in the name of God is poetry for?
I'll have ye know we've sunk to a truthless lot.
I'd scorn to damp my feet in this tadpole pond,"
Said the wild old woman who was never bewildered.

Said the old woman, "Don't forget I knew
That giant among all the men of my youth.
And knew the beauty queen who tramped his heart.
But it was me—never her—understood his poems,"
Said the old woman angry with the world.

Said the old woman, slugging herself again,
"'More geese than swans now live, more fools than wise.'
An Elizabethan sang that stave for us.
My time was all guts and brains and I've outlived it,"
Said the old woman shaking her bottle at the flooding wind.

Paging Mr. Paterson

for William Carlos Williams

On this day I was born
Forty-eight years ago.
And what's it to you? or me?

I sit in a little house.
I can see on the sun outside
Apricot blossoming white
And the pink-blossoming peach
In cold mountain air.
I have come this far, this high,
From the slow hill of birth.

I have read the morning away
With an old man's youngest poem
Made in his seventy-fifth year—
A time when all is one—
To say that virgin and whore
Are as one, and Art is all:
The poem become at last
A vast meadow of flowers,
A brave dance of Yes.

That old man, mad for words.

I recall the day I said
"I am twelve! I am twelve! I am twelve!"
That day I knew I was twelve.
Who knows now what I am?
Or how far I have come?
But closer to this hawk-high sun.

I should like to send these trees,
White and pink over black,

To the old man, to say
"Here, these are all for you."
And: "Neither you nor I
Are in the habit of prayer;
So will you *wish* me then
For the year I am seventy-five
The meadow, the measured dance."

I watch the flowered branches.
They curve to my one desire.
They bend toward my last desire.

3: The Man at Mid-Century

The Man at Mid-Century

We cannot guess how long he'll wait.
He paces in his room alone
Imagining someone must come
Whose voice will force the lag of fate.
He paces puzzled, helpless, dumb,
Or sits beside the telephone
Hoping it may ring his ring
And someone solve him everything.
Television, radio:
Sessions to watch and listen to
Lest someone there let slip the clue
Of what he needs to need to know.
All possibilities allowed,
He leaves the latchkeys in his locks
And walks among the city crowd
Seeking the face that will reveal
Someone whose quickening answers frame
His inarticulate questioning.
He hurries home to letter-box,
To rooms as empty, to the same
Expectancy of dreams and drink.
Pacing he waits for me or you
Or anyone to speak his name:
Someone to tell him what to do
Someone to tell him what to think
Someone to tell him what to feel

Unfurnished Room

You stand alone in an emptied house
And stare from the sill into a vacant room:
Wallpaper whirls around the gaping closet.
The six-over-six windows to the east
Are reproduced at slant across the floor.
So this is morning, of a clear day.
Your heart, the only sound, accelerates
Because nothing yet has happened to you here
Or everything has happened and is over.

Two

There was that fall the fall of desire
And in the senseless night a sense of wires
Cut, plugs pulled from the darkened switchboard;
And then the silent cold like unspoken words,
And then the snow silencing depths and heights.
Together we walked alone the white-twigged night
Followed by our desperate, disparate tracks
Which even to us were lost when we looked back.

The Wrong Is Mixed

Can cockcrow fix a landscape?
Morning anywhere in the world.
Country nostalgias. Here is
Season of spiders, webs before wind.
Blue air curved yellow with fruit,
Green disintegrates: decomposition
Is peaceful. Dove wings rising
Clap an applause of peace.
At early crow, light's a long level.

We hear that the world will end;
What heart believes it? We hear of
Beginningless and endless universe;
What mind imagines it? And if
We are unwebbed and the wind comes
That blows the world away, betrayed
From green for the last time—cockcrow
Must cry up that tearing air like
Memory of the morning of the world.

Here on water, one scarlet leaf for love.

What I Assembled and Dissemble

What I assembled and dissemble
Mix and merge in this bird-drenched wood.
What I invent and what remember
Will never save me from the sod.

Those held loving and those abandoned
Sigh together when I am gone.
Under the grass is understanding:
Ash in a jar, *I-told-you-so.*

Every lilac that blossomed is
In this one flower—take it for yours.
Such fragrance gives so brief a blessing
That all my Mays come back in tears.

Surf of wind on the willow-walk,
This fluttering shuttle of flying song,
Mean what the cherry's white floating fall
Means to morning: We knew this once.

We are deep tranced in repetition
Having ourselves the frailest sum—
Forgetting, forever young in passion,
How useless is the lie of rhyme.

The Long Party

Identification had to be by mask.
The party went on so long. So long.
Nobody bared a face. All those lanterns.
It was maggot-time in the blood trees. Even
Above the sludge of the sea that other sound
Ate among us in crepitant whispers.
A few desperate errors aside, there were
No real connections; woman with woman,
Man with man; relief was agitating.
"I am too old to dance," said an old man:
"Will you dance for me?" To somebody young.
I'd have sworn nobody was there. Dark.
Hopefully: "Old people for contrast at a party.
But there's no such thing," he said, "as a hundred years."
In the dusk the children sat discussing death.
Later they were gone—too late—to bed.
A wilder surf of music. That—I thought—
First sounded in a skull two-hands-sized,
Now it roves the sky. But these were maskers
Knew how to dance without hearing the music.
Where the children had hidden I stumbled
Scattering a pattern of letter-blocks
Though in that light I doubt I could have read.
The lawn sloped down to the blue hydrangeas,
The blue hydrangeas held the sea. Apart,
I found a clump of laurel I remembered:
But shriveled. I had dreamed that laurel tall.

The Hour Is Late

It seemed to me in the night
I had no art after all.
That all I had tried to make
Was never for its own sake,
Stank with impurity,
And that what my enemies said
My kind friends left unsaid.
Then it seemed to me
I stumbled in a dark hall
In an unfamiliar house
Where I had no business to be.

Did vanity espouse
Such self-deceiving as mine?
As though not tree but vine—
As though not girl but kiss—
Were the reality.
Or had I at first some reason?
The beginning as true for me
As for some luckier men
Who quarried the light of day
Out of such night as this?

There was nothing to which to pray,
And the night was very late.
I could neither love nor hate
Who had lived so long alone
With an invented ghost
That now was utterly gone.
A naked man in a strange house
In the dark, nameless and lost.

The Fall

The stilted beetle steps
Through the leaf-muddled grass.
Branch by branch, yellow
Stains down the poplar trees.

The dusty spiders slink
Into the house. The wind
Sleets across windowpanes
The lilacs' blackened leaves.

In erosion's work
We hide the name of love,
And remember rain
Down the strangers' streets.

No grief is annual.
We smell our blackened hearts
Unseasonably hurt
With their unflaking char.

Foul weather was fair
For poetry and love.
Now without prizes—
As most dogs do—we live.

The old men arrive
Who have the world in charge
And are about to leave.
They toss it carelessly

To the moon and back.
Perhaps. In carelessness
Born of a surety
Fire is posthumous.

We know now that our tears
Are always for ourselves.
We stomp the spiders flat.
The beetle chill's unfelt.

All our news is death.
Clowns are dangerous.
We have proved paradise
The illusion of our eyes.

Watch Hill

Unsexed by the cold sea, prone out of it on the beach,
Too diminished for art, I yet resolving
To write only of seasons other than the present,
To try the imagination, the larger love;
All the while the sanded wind blew over me.

Next-naked the young woman on her back
Slept brown and gold along a blue blanket,
Her children near; I spied upon her thighs
Forked open and the mount of glossy ribs and
All the while the sanded wind blew over her.

Two children small and gold who bucketed,
Built and bashed at variance, and now
Trotted with new knees to borrow some ocean,
Then peered to find if their mother still slept;
All the while the sanded wind blew past them.

Strangers, we three shared an altering patience;
I at my distance beginning to fondle a daydream
On that upturned, abandoned face, and they
Running in close to see when it would claim them,
All the while the sanded wind blew past it.

Their play dropped, sudden as fright among birds
They pounced, calling, shaking and waking her;
I closed my eyes upon her; the plunge and plunge
Of stroking ocean remotely hot and swollen,
And all the while the sanded wind blew between us.

Blue Sleigh

Blue sleigh that fifty winters gone
Swan-breasted heavier snows than ours,
Arrested on your summer lawn
Stands filled with earth and planted flowers.

Its shafts slant empty to the ground
As if they'd never held a horse;
Its runners make the breathless sound
Allotted rust and ghosts, of course.

The flowers are white geranium.
Stuck in June grass it looks as though
Somehow the sleigh had tunneled home
Through one immortal drift of snow.

Present preservative of past?
That what it raced through it contains?
But your illusion will not last:
Here's white geranium and it stains.

You lover of the incongruous:
Better to have your blue sleigh drawn
Through all those daisy fields across
The hills to time's malignant sun.

Exercise in Aesthetics

The lilac bushes were small with winter.
Rain-repeated, the abacus of barberries
Ran red, ran red above the smoking snow
And the green chickweed where it winked.
Low to the ground, fog hovered and blew and shifted.
The house we passed was three miles from the last
And, as it turned out, three miles from the next.
A back road between cold-blackened pines
On a cellar of a morning near December's end.
Nobody visible at the house. My question was
Whom were all the Christmas signals for—
The candles in the windows and the doorwreath
Ribboned to render hemlock a gay creation?
At most a stranger or two passed once a day,
Like us, in a moment passing. For us, then?
Yes, if we happened by. But of necessity
First for the mingled joy of decoration
And whoever made it. How else could it be?

The Double Tree

I do not know why. It is not only
In the April sun the flowered apricot tree—
It is more the shadow of the tree against the wall
The shadow of flowered branches that sets the tree
There in the April sun and on the earth,
Fan coral within the soft sea of spring.
Sparrow and the shadow of sparrow fly
Into the double tree, create it there
So dimensional it must be believed.
What sun objectifies, like us, is real
For this little while in the sun's season.

Obdurate Change

Leaves falling falling in the woods
Make a rainy sound across the sun.

All sift and wavering of leaves and shift
Of light—the woods opening everywhere.

Have we names now, walking alone together,
So far from everyone, as two together?

No leaf is the same for any other's eye:
No name is the same, even for you and me.

Leaves falling falling in the woods.
Sun on so many names, the names on stones.

And the stones changing in the mutable air,
Planes of light sliding, melting, re-forming.

The woods walk through us season over season.
Walking their leaves we make the sound of fall.

From Chirico to Charon

Vacancies of Chirico Square repeated as far as Charon's River;
The River invisible from here.
Stone line of the houses empty also; staring, he somehow knew;
By, perhaps, a buttressing vibrance hollowing noon to an unreal
    moonlight,
Zero parthenogenesis ordered inevitably;
And a pack of dry leaves, squeaking wind-driven, crossing the
    road like rats.

To walk inward—to begin to diminish; and he began; slowly.

By the moving assumed the strength, made of a braid of his
    weaknesses,
And his discovery of this; as he changed, gospels occurred and
    were birds around him
And he continued steadily and unhindered;
In his progress was his living, and its direction certain
Now he accomplished the one defense against general disaster:
    imagined his death.

Vanished beyond the Square he arrived at the River;
Of the coin of his life he could not tell the value, but rejoiced
    at the light weight of it in his mouth.

Between Ironwood and the Sea

The sand around the ironwood
And the ironwood remain an alien place.
Though I have watched remotest land
Close in snow to a remembered field
This goes, like dreams slept out.
Daylight is the world.

Buckhorn twists in the lilac shoots.
Where last year's oak leaves lock
There is the prickly pear.
Against the adobe wall
Hollyhocks sway with bees.
And then the rain punctual upon dust
Becomes nostalgic acid on the tongue,
Then lids the day and fills the air
With dark and lilac-loaded cold.

Black mesa and the Merrimack
Adjacent in the darkened dream
Split in the daylight world
Till each man move between
Salt womb and ironwood
Sea and desert, the breathless places.
Only between them marriage happens.

Here in the youngest land
Whose yucca roots in rock, whose rock
Is a rage of fire stilled to iron,
We walk that earth where the sea
Most lately was.
Here in stone is the backbone of a fish
Here the rendered fern:
The difference within the resemblances
Holds all our art and joy and grief.

On hard clay shaped ten hundred years
By the bare tread of the nerved foot,
I saw the old men who used to dance
Chanting and drumming for the virile dancers
Who were aped by children
Wavering in evergreens;
And the possible sanity of life
Seemed the very sun over them,
And I who could never dance for it
Wept for joy.

Everything sifts from the human hand
Like dust, like water.
A mix of the two can be shaped
And reshaped in sameness with a difference forever.
Look! I had been told
There could be snow on the blossoming lilac.
I have seen it now and stayed
Because it is so.

The Blue Tree

The leaves fell all from the tree.
The birds flew into it
And made for a while a blue tree.
They were jays—sarah and piñon jays:
Could perch intensely blue
And fly it intenser still:
Out they went as on strings
Circling, clustering in again.
Green the tree had been; then gold—
For days gold; now a moment blue.

Winter was beginning to come.
Snow on the mountains. From houses
All the blue doors in the wind clapped
"Hail Mary! Hail Mary!"
The sun sang like wires everywhere.
I, in another's dream—a strange country
Which belonged to me though not I to it:
I could speak, but got no answers.

If I grow old—I came to know this—
The world I die from can never be
The world most mine. Green given,
Gold from green; but then
The blue, temporary tree.
To love is to stay, and that
Will have been another place and season.
The tree flies green to somebody's other dream.

Love and a Season

Over what freshets of light on April mornings
Robins burble their six-note seesaw-song—
Elm-high above blue damp shadows and valley mist
A prestidigitation, a fountained waste
Of juggled gold that only May will match
With dandelion fields' prodigal silence
Beyond the spume of May.
                                        And now farewell
To the June town of ladies in cotton lilac
Bending their frail look upon picketed iris
In hopelessly joined grids of scented yards
That give on the valley view that gives on graves
Tucked in the north corner of the sky. Farewell
That little way down hill to the terraced stillness
Where mosspink stitches the anonymous scars
To a brave indifference of forgetfulness
Under this music thinned and long familiar
Which is not yet exactly mine, for the grave—transfixed,
Oh, my loved ghost!—most mine is not among these
And the house I have to go home to is a new house.

N. M.

Walking over the loma and down to the arroyo
In the windy weather of the year the time the world
Melts to spring and here dries thin in the smashing sun,
I might have descended cliffs of the moon to an old sea floor.

And parasitical suck in the cedars like green sea-sponge
Flecked pink, emblem of kisses, polyp-building, coral-
Budding, mistletoe writhed to its skeletal achievement.
I saw on the sand two lovers knotting their naked sprawl.

I saw moving steadily, earth into sky, like the conjugal
Hyphen a single plane bagged heavy with seed of death.
Amongst these and upright with my choice I chose
Where to be lonely to learn to tell mountains from clouds.

Light Enough to Go Round

New perceptions—even light-houses
can throw them far inland. . . .
—Haniel Long

The light that wheels through night
To guide the ships at sea,
One third of its turning light
Seems burning uselessly.

Two thirds of the time it keeps
Its vigil on rocks and waves
But each time round it sweeps
Over houses, fields and graves
Where its light may waken some
Who don't yet sleep too hard.

In necessitous go-and-come
With nothing inland to guard
It abandons indifferently
The seaborne to helplessness
And plays ghost from trinity
Upon those it need not bless.

It is never at once a wheel—
This succession of points in round
Which flash toward hull and keel.

Still it has to swing overground
To swing at all and agree
With required shape of earth
And how life and death must be
And love and birth.

To Earth

I died but woke again
Lying on summer ground
Looking up through a tree
At sunlight in green leaves
Where speckle-dappled birds
Played the black branches.

When I was very young
I learned how black can shine
By husking beady seeds
Out of columbine pods:
Black mica or birds' eyes
Are not a shinier black.

Consider, furthermore,
That these are seeds outwhispering
Dry, dead urns—
And poured into the earth
Will ascend again
And descend like doves

In white and purple clusters
Every next spring's sun
Hovering like small doves;
That Harlequin also
Is dappled: lives and dies
And lives—like us—and laughs.

Looking up through the tree
I saw all shining sun
Intermittent with leaves
No less than the bird-song
And buttress-branched across
As I had loved it most.

Bermuda Suite

1: The Voyage

The gray the vacant circle of the sea
Port and starboard sways among the clouds.
Like a slow metronome for timelessness
The centered ship creaks deeply down the east
Then slides against the west to tilt on clouds
That hold all this lolling quicksilver.

And thus eternity except for us;
Though keeled and waked obliterative in foam
Our interceptions of this pulsing void
Grew its existence and inhabitants,
And with salt tongue and all-pervading eye
Named the pastures of leviathan.

Marked by multitudinous hoofs of the wind
The waters of the world before the world
Have now become the landless skyless world,
And gray and cold and dumb and meaningless
Save for the mastery of our prow, and that
Advancing always rolls dead center still.

Southeast where morning showed beyond the prow,
Only the intermittent flaws in cloud—
Which mend and darken with a chilling zeal—
Admit light's vibrant archipelagoes.
Their brief creations on the ocean flash
Like glittering ghostly islands of the sun.

2: The Green Moray

Fourteen miles off the land the sharp reefs fissure the water
and at low-tide the water splits white on the coral bone;
None does, but a man could walk here.

What lurks here, deep and obscure in the swilling waters, is
the great eel, the green moray.

This reef-arch, vertebrae revealed, locked skeletons where the
volcanic spew shuddering away failed northwest to achieve
One island more,—
This guards the Eden of hibiscus, floating Bermudas, crescent
of strung barges of flowers between the cobalt air and the
zircon-melted sea.
All those islands in a dust of gold
Strewing on water their harebell-haunted hills
That change from morning to evening from blue to mauve,
Staked with cedar, paved with lily, branched with palm, and
breathing freesia
Under the singing rings of scarlet birds.

Toward those the green moray lifts an indifferent eye long-
learned in patient hate; slow and watchful amidst coral
Shifts the thick mass of his cold length;
Coiled in the dead defenses of the reefs he waits vicious for
millennium,
When from the grottoes worms the landward march of the
fathom-hidden,
Innumerable in a sluggish final seminal wave.

3: Portrait of Lizards

The lizard on the limestone wall
Shifts a noncommittal eye,
Innocently prehistorical.

Miss Moore remarked his heavy clay:
Miniature dinosaurian,
Ownerless, immortal toy.

Rust on cedar, blue on stone,
Green-mottle to the yucca spikes,
He poses frozen in the sun.

All afternoon is how he likes
Baking on his chilly buff:
So we assume: that what it takes

To stay so everlasting tough
Is thus desiring heat and light
While never getting quite enough.

He has not climbed far from the sight
And sound and savor of the sea,
Yet he has compromised the night

With undivulged facility.
He scuttles where the cacti sprawl
Across the rock; amidst them, he

Mounts a dome of brain coral:
There, self-fixed, triumphant, small,
The lizard's portrait of a moral . . .

Cold, chameleon, inexplicable.

4: Kites, Good Friday

Upon mine honor, sir, I heard a humming,
And that a strange one too, which did awake me.
—The Tempest

Seven little boys like silhouettes dancing far on the headland
Salute the morning with the running and the rising of their
kites.
Uphill, drawing them, the soft brown hands
paying out string,
The boys have set them swinging in the wind on a rag-tailed
rocking and rising
And riding with a surge higher and east toward the sun and out on
Tauter string over the sea–far–stretched–rigid now–
anchored and almost stilled
Stiffly balancing wind: each octagonal kite like a burning gem

Purple and gold and red; seal-centered with–invisibly–the
bright paper heart;
The humming beginning now out of the strung-wedged V's, a high
keening across the Good Friday sun;
And cries on and on.

Swiftly by ancient custom all over the
Bermuda islands
The sky fills–thousands of many-colored kites staining like
marvels of windows the great blue air.
The sky sways with the glass of God, the whole dome throbbing
with massed fretting of jewels, and their crying
Motored now to a diapason pulse, a humming roar drowning the
wind;
And looped over the white shores and the outer reefs the foams
Break without sound.

In this blazing dazzle of color
all heaven moans
Reels in this spangling of spectrum; the air imbued
Purple and gold and red: ascending and singing day-dream strung
From the thousands of soft hands that have set sounding together
Multitudinous wires, space-filling harp tilting its mineral
fires slant to the sun,
All fragmented are joined and woven, transformed, and the sky
opening with transfigured blood.

Between all lifted hands and the kites such intense power strains,
Which holds? Which is held?
The power flows up the strings into the sky out of the hands
that have set this glory there,
All faces lifted to love what they have made.
Even all the islands for this little while
Lifted between the waters and the sky.

5: Long. 64° 50′ W; Lat. 32° 15′ N

Flared down from broken cloud the calipered light
Stood strident, made exact embrace of land.
Brooched crescent upon platinum the islands
Curved gold-flecked emerald, and there was light
Only along the great bow of the islands
As though they swung burning alone in space.

Running out of the sea the man and woman
Flashed on the shore naked and beautiful,
And flung to sand as by a wave of air
They lay together breathlessly and then
They heard their hearts, and time resumed its beat.
Sand kept flickering with the ticking wind.

The sand swept high to a long wave of earth
That, wrought upon the rock, had rooted rock
Tendrilled in a gigantic grasp from air
Holding in perilous suspension
What cragged mass the sea once lifted up,
Conjoined from accident this miracle.

At its emergent line the man and woman
Stared at cloud-vexed sky, the chains of light.
They saw the flowered headlands shake and quiet
In crisscross hammering of their sea-lashed hearts,
And remembered in wild wonder-eaten wisdom
That all the flowering was meant for them.

Coleridge

Old father, blessed ghost, mariner
Of my launching, fixer of the bloody sun
Round which my condemned and lifelong voyage
Swerves and follows—follows again, ignorant
What tropic oceans, what icy straits
Hide ahead, or winds across the magnet
Shudder deeper than engines, or tides
Trouble the ways before the invisible pole
Set under that unsetting sun;

old talker

Glittering through my childhood—voice and eyes
Compellent to hold, to send me out to
Find home by way of Vinland, India, by
Horns of undiscovered coasts that sounded
Music undeniable till the sea
Flamed with mirage that grayed all gold;

old

Detective of death in the boy's hand in the lane—
Resolve my life again. By this invocation
Invoke me—blessed ghost, old father.